YARRA LIBRARIES

G000146308

HELBLING LANGUAGES

www.helblinglanguages.com

Ricky and the American Girl
by Martyn Hobbs
© HELBLING LANGUAGES 2007

All rights reserved. No part of this publication may be reproduced, stored in a retrieval system, or transmitted, in any form or by any means, electronic, mechanical, photocopying, recording, or otherwise, without the prior written permission of the publishers.

First published 2007

ISBN 978-3-902504-20-3

Series editor Maria Cleary
Illustrated by Lorenzo Sabbatini
Activities by Elspeth Rawstron
Design and layout by Capolinea
Printed by Athesia

About this Book

For the Student

🎧 Listen to all of the story and do some activities on your Audio CD

▷◁ Talk about the story

bits• When you see the blue dot you can check the word in the glossary on page 62

For the Teacher

Go to our Readers Resource site for information on using readers and downloadable Resource Sheets, photocopiable Worksheets, Answer Keys and Tapescripts. Plus the full version of the story on MP3.

www.helblinglanguages.com/readers

For lots of great ideas on using Graded Readers consult Reading Matters, the Teacher's Guide to using Helbling Readers.

Level 3 Structures

Present continuous for future	Cardinal / ordinal numbers
Present perfect	One / ones
Present perfect versus past simple	Reflexive pronouns
Should / shouldn't (advice and obligation)	Indefinite pronouns
Must / should	
Need to / have to	Too plus adjective
Will	Not plus adjective plus enough
	Relative pronouns who, which and that
Ever / never	Prepositions of time, place and movement
Would like	
So do I / neither do I	
Question tags	

Structures from lower levels are also included

Contents

Before Reading

1 Look at the picture and answer the questions on pages 8 and 9.

Before Reading

1 Talk about parties. Ask and answer these questions with a partner.

    a) Have you ever been to a fireworks party?
    b) When? Where? Who with?
    c) What was the last party you went to?
    d) What was it like?
    e) Did you meet anyone interesting?

2 Find these things in the picture and label them.

a) bonfire	c) leather jacket	e) guy
b) firework	d) sausage	f) chicken drumsticks

3 In groups write a story about a fireworks party. It can be a romance, a detective story or a thriller. Include as many of the things in exercise 2 as you can. Tell the story to the class and choose the best one.

4 Listen and find Alexis, Ricky, Holly and Grace in the picture. Write their names.

5 Answer the questions.

a) What is Alexis wearing?

....

b) What nationality is Alexis?

....

c) What is Holly doing?

....

d) What is Grace eating?

....

e) What is Ricky doing?

....

f) What is on top of the bonfire?

....

6 Can you guess?

What will happen between Ricky and Alexis?
Will they go on a date?
Will it go well? Why? Why not?

7 Plan a date for two of the characters in the picture with a partner. Then tell the class.

Ricky's world changed completely on a cold Friday afternoon in November.

It was only five to four but it was already getting dark. Ricky was walking home from school, his bag hanging• over his shoulder. He wasn't listening to his MP3 or chatting with friends. He was alone and he was doing calculations in his head – maths calculations. He was a bit of a mathematical genius• and he loved solving problems. He didn't need a calculator or a computer. He could do them in his head.

But then he saw someone looking up and down the street. She seemed confused. But when she saw Ricky, she called out. And from that moment on, his life would never be the same again.

Ricky's week started normally enough.

On Monday morning at breakfast time, while he was trying to read his computer games magazines, he had to listen to his sisters' favourite topic● of conversation – boys.

'You can't like Steve, he's so ordinary,' said Sonia.
'He's really good-looking,' said Jade.
'Good-looking? No, Hassan's good-looking ...'
'No way●!'
'And Ryan,' continued Sonia, 'and Tyler and Sam.'
'Yes, Sam has lovely hair,' agreed Jade. 'And Tyler wears cool clothes.'
'Yeah, and Ryan's a good dancer,' added Sonia. 'And not many boys can dance!'
They started laughing.
'You should learn to dance, Ricky,' said Jade. 'Then you might get a girlfriend.'
Ricky blushed●. And then they laughed some more.

On Tuesday, Ricky spent the whole evening in his room working at his computer. On Tuesday his class always had maths homework and Ricky always helped out his schoolmates● with their problems. They sent him emails asking him for advice●, and he emailed them back with suggestions and explanations. He never actually● told them the answers – Ricky was too honest for that – but he guided them in the right direction to find the solutions for themselves. He didn't charge● for the service, either, although Jack often pointed out●, 'You could make a lot of money doing this.' But Ricky enjoyed helping his friends.

Ricky was always a bit of a hero on Wednesdays. His friends went up to him and thanked him for his help with their homework.

'Hey, Ricky, you were brilliant!' said Josh.

'Thanks, man,' said Dan.

'You're another Einstein!' said Alex.

Ricky saw Jack kicking a ball around the school yard.

'Hi, Jack,' Ricky said.

Jack looked at him and nodded.

'Have you done your maths homework?' Ricky asked.

Jack shook his head.

'Do you want me to take a look?'

Jack didn't have a computer at home, and he didn't like to ask for anything. Jack nodded and smiled.

'OK. We've got ten minutes!'

Teachers liked Ricky, too, especially the maths and science ones. Whenever● they asked questions, Ricky always seemed to know the answers.

When Mr Edwards asked a question like, 'What happens when we add sulphuric acid to ...?' most of the class didn't listen to the end of the sentence. It was either too boring or too difficult to follow. Ricky was different. He knew the answer even before Mr Edwards finished.

And when Ms Cooke wrote '$4x + 2(y - z) =?$' Ricky knew what number x represented●. He knew what y was. He even understood what z meant. Alex was right. Ricky really was a genius!

Friday was a cold and miserable day. But everyone was happy as the school bell rang and it was time to go home. The weekend started now!

Ricky heard brief bits* of conversation as he walked across the playground. David was arranging to see Jack on Saturday afternoon. Josh was talking quietly to Anna. And Holly was talking to Zadie and Grace.

'What are you doing at the weekend, Holly?' asked Grace.
'Oh, well, it's going to be fun. We've got relatives staying and...'
But Ricky didn't hear what Holly was going to do. As he got to the gates, Dan and Alex called out, 'See you, Ricky!'

'Bye', said Ricky, and set off* home.

Ricky turned up* the collar of his blazer*. It was cold and damp* and it was already getting dark. He was walking home alone. It was strange, Ricky was popular with the boys in his class, but he wasn't close friends with any of them. And although he was good-looking, and girls sometimes whispered* things about him and giggled*, he didn't hang out with them either. He was happy with his own company. He had his own website; he invented computer games; and he composed music on his PC. He also enjoyed doing calculations in his head. Which was what he was doing at 15:55 when he saw a girl standing in the road ahead of him.

Ricky watched her walking away down the road. He was still standing under the streetlight when she looked back and gave a little wave. Ricky waved back. And then she was gone.

'Oh, no!' sighed Ricky. 'I didn't ask her name!'

On Friday evenings Ricky usually worked on his computer. This Friday evening was different. He was restless•.

'Are you OK, Ricky?' asked his sister Jade who was putting on make-up.

'What?' he replied.

'Is your computer broken?' asked Sonia who was putting in earrings.

'No,' he said.

'So what's up?•' she asked.

'Nothing.'

Ricky didn't know what to say.

When the front door closed behind his two sisters, Ricky went into the sitting room. His parents were watching TV. They looked up, surprised to see him. He hardly ever watched TV.

'Oh no, a stupid quiz programme,' thought Ricky. But he sat on the sofa and watched it with them. And then a sitcom● started that wasn't funny at all. And then it was time for the news. Ricky sighed.

'Are you all right, Ricky?' his mother asked.

'I'm fine,' he replied.

'Don't forget, you're helping in the shop tomorrow,' said his father, looking up from his newspaper.

'I haven't forgotten,' said Ricky. 'I guess I'll go to bed now.'

But when he went to bed, he couldn't sleep. First he lay on one side, then he lay on the other. He lay on his back. That was hopeless. So he tried his front – and that was worse. He looked at his digital alarm clock. It said 23:45 in bright red numbers. Ricky tossed and turned• until the clock said 01:27. And the next thing he knew, he was walking through a strange city with tall skyscrapers• and big flashy• cars. It was a warm sunny day. Everyone else was wearing T-shirts and light summer clothes. For some reason he had on his school uniform and he felt hot and uncomfortable. A small boy looked at him and laughed.

Ricky turned a corner and found himself standing on a beach. The clean yellow sand stretched away into the distance. The sea was a brilliant blue with long white waves. He was the only person there. He took off his shoes and socks, rolled up• his trousers, and walked towards the cool water. And then he realized he wasn't alone. A girl was walking on the wet sand. She was paddling in the water. Her hair was blond and shone in the sunlight. Ricky tried to call out to her but he had no voice. How could he get her attention? But then, slowly, she turned her head towards him. It was the American girl. And she smiled.

And then his alarm clock beeped angrily and he woke up.

On Saturdays, Ricky often helped at his parents' shop. He normally didn't mind• and they gave him some money which he always spent on computer software or games. But today was strange. He wanted to be somewhere else. He wanted to do something different. Unfortunately, he didn't know what.

He was sitting on his knees, putting some magazines on a shelf, when he heard a voice outside. Was it Holly? It sounded like her. Then he heard another voice, a voice full of sunshine, a voice with an American accent.

Was it her? Was it the American girl? He stood up and looked out of the window but there was nobody there.

'They're walking away from the shop,' he thought. 'There's still time. I can call out to them!'

Ricky rushed to the door. But he stopped suddenly before he stepped outside. 'What am I doing?' he asked himself. 'What will I say to her if I see her? She isn't on her own. She could be with Holly – if that was Holly's voice.'

And then he thought, 'Holly? With the American girl? How can she be with her?' He tried to remember the conversation he heard when he was leaving school. Holly was talking about her plans for the weekend. What did she say? Ricky had a great memory for facts, he was famous for his memory. But his memory couldn't help him now.

'What are you doing?' his father asked behind him.

Ricky turned, he was blushing. He didn't know what to say.

'Come on, get back to work.'

NEWSAGENT

WESTBOURNE
NEWS

Westbourne
Girls win
soccer match!

Ricky didn't do anything interesting for the rest of the weekend. In fact, he couldn't think of anything interesting to do. He surfed the net – but he wasn't looking for anything. He watched TV – but he didn't remember anything. He listened to his sisters' conversations – but he didn't say anything. Ricky was only doing one thing. He was waiting for the weekend to finish and for the new school week to start. He wanted to see Holly. He wanted to know about the American girl. And on Monday morning, he didn't have long to wait.

Ricky watched Holly from the moment he arrived at school. She talked a little to Grace, but he couldn't hear what they said. He went over to talk to her but the bell rang. Then lessons started and he didn't have a chance to discover anything.

But at 10:30, Holly made an announcement●. It was too cold and miserable● to go outside during the break, so they were sitting around the classroom.
Holly said, 'I'm going to have a party on Saturday.'
They looked up. A party, near the end of November, the most boring time of the year? This was great news!
'Yeah,' she continued, 'We're going to have a fireworks● party.'

'A fireworks party?' said Grace. 'You're a bit late for fireworks, aren't you?'

'Guy Fawkes was two weeks ago,' added David.

'Where have you been? In the jungle?' asked Zadie.

'Very funny. Not,' said Holly, smiling.

'Do we have to eat veggie• burgers – or can we have sausages, too?' asked Jack.

'No veggie burgers, please,' groaned• everyone.

Everyone called Holly the 'eco warrior' because she was a vegetarian and because she was always worrying about the state of the planet•. Actually, everyone agreed with Holly (about the state of the planet, not about food), but they liked teasing• her just the same•.

'Actually,' said Holly, 'I've got my cousin staying with me ...'

Ricky suddenly felt hot, then cold.
'A cousin?' thought Ricky.
'She's here with my uncle and aunt ...'
'Holly said 'she'', thought Ricky. 'So her cousin's a girl ... '
His throat went dry. He had to swallow•.
'They live in America,' added Holly.
'America!' thought Ricky. His heart started pounding•, the room started spinning•, and he heard a weird• buzzing in his head.
'It's her! It's the girl in the road ... so it was them outside my parents' shop.'
'And we wanted to do something fun,' said Holly. 'She's never been to a Guy Fawkes party before. So we're going to have a guy, and a bonfire ... the whole thing!'

'That's a great idea!' said Zadie. 'What time will it start?'

'Oh, at about five,' said Holly. 'Can you all come?'

Everyone said 'yes', including Ricky. In fact, he said 'yes' very loudly. He almost shouted it.

Everyone turned to look at him.

'Are you going to come to my party?' asked Holly. She was surprised.

'Erm ... yes, if that's all right.'

'Of course it's all right!' she said, and gave him a nice smile.

Jack looked at Ricky.

'I don't get it●,' he said. 'You never go to parties!'

'I know,' said Ricky, 'but ... well, I'd like to go to this one. I like fireworks. And Guy Fawkes ... and ...'

Ricky didn't know what to say. Jack laughed. And then the teacher walked in and it was time for English.

That week, Ricky's life passed in a strange dream. It wasn't exactly pleasant•, but it wasn't unpleasant either. He found that, for the first time in his life, he listened to the words of silly love songs. And he didn't find them silly any more –the words made sense.

He spent hours looking though his wardrobe trying to decide what to wear to the party. He tried all his clothes on, took them off, tried them on again. He finally decided on a purple shirt. It was quite trendy• and it looked good with his dark skin and hair.

And he listened to the conversations of his sisters and tried, again for the first time in his life, to understand what girls were really like.

At last, the days and hours finally passed, and it was half past four on Saturday. Ricky was wearing his purple shirt and new blue jeans. He looked at himself in the mirror and combed his hair for the twenty-first time that day. He put on his leather jacket and he tried to smile at his reflection. He couldn't. His legs were weak. His hands started shaking•.

He tried to say 'hello' to his reflection and no sound came out. He felt sick with nerves. He looked at the clock. It was a quarter to five. Feeling like a prisoner on death row• who was about to be executed•, Ricky opened his bedroom door, and walked downstairs.

Everybody was at Holly's party. The house was full, the back garden was full, even the garage was full! Ricky pushed through the crowd, looking for the American girl. There were girls with red hair, brown hair, black hair, blond hair – but nobody had the beautiful long blond hair of the American girl.

'Hey, great shirt!' shouted David.

'Thanks!' said Ricky. 'Erm ... have you seen ... ?'

Then Ricky thought, 'I can't say the American girl! I still don't know her name!'

'Holly?' said David. 'Yeah, she's in the garden with Alexis.'

'Alexis,' thought Ricky. 'What a beautiful name.'

Suddenly Jack shouted in their ears.

'Come on, it's time for the fireworks!'

And they rushed into the garden.

The fireworks exploded in a blaze of colour. Everybody looked up at the colourful patterns as they lit up the sky. Everyone except Ricky. He was looking at Alexis. For him, her hair was brighter and lovelier than the fireworks.
Ricky tried to talk to Alexis ... but it wasn't easy. There were always people in the way.

Ricky didn't have another chance to talk to her. There were too many people in the way. So he chatted to David and listened to Jack and talked to Holly. She was very friendly and happy to see him at the party. But Ricky's thoughts were on Alexis. He didn't like all those boys around her. But she liked his shirt. She said his purple shirt was cute!

At home, he didn't say much when his sisters asked him about the party. But he was always thinking about it, and about Alexis. He kept looking for her on Monday on his way to and from school.

And then on Tuesday after school, there she was ...

On the corner by the school, Alexis was talking to Holly and Grace. Ricky walked slowly towards them.

'I'm busy this weekend,' Holly was saying. 'I've got to write up my project and I haven't even started yet!'

'I don't know anything about a project,' thought Ricky.

Then Alexis said, 'Do you want my cell phone number, Grace?'

'Oh, sure,' said Grace.

'It's 087 5664 7861.'

'Hi!' said Ricky in a nervous voice.

The girls looked round at him.

'Oh, hi Ricky.'

Alexis gave a little smile.

And Ricky walked on past, his heart pounding.

He was repeating a number to himself: '087 5664 7861.'

He could remember her mobile phone number!

For the rest of the week, Ricky couldn't sleep. When he closed his eyes, eleven numbers burned in the darkness. When he tried to do maths, eleven numbers filled his brain. When his sisters talked to him at breakfast, eleven numbers filled his ears. He didn't know what to do.

He knew her mobile phone number. He knew Holly was busy at the weekend – and he knew Alexis was free. He could call her. He could speak to her and arrange* to meet. But every time he decided to do it, he couldn't press the call button.

Finally, at 1:48 a.m. on Saturday morning, he wrote a text message.

> HI
> I CAN SHOW YOU AROUND TOWN TODAY IF YOU WANT.
> RICKY

But he felt worse* than ever.

'What have I done?' he thought, as he lay sleepless* in bed.

'What have I done?' he asked himself, as he washed in the morning.

'What have I done?' he groaned, as he couldn't eat his breakfast.

'Are you OK?' asked Jade.

'You look terrible,' said Sonia.

'Don't go to the shop today,' said his mother. 'You should relax!'

Ricky nodded. 'I didn't remember the shop!' he thought.

And then he heard a beep from his phone. There was a message. He opened it nervously. It only contained* one word:

> SURE

Alexis didn't like his favourite shops. She was bored by computers and she never read books.
And this one's my favourite game ...
Do you like the colour of my nails? It's a cute pink, isn't it?
So Ricky took her to the park. There was a view of the town and the river.
This is my favourite place. I like sitting up here.
Really? What do you do?
Well, I ... I think a lot, and I like looking out over the town ...
It's a very small town.
Well, it isn't very big ...
Not very big? It's tiny! And it's also very cold.
Oh, OK ...
Ricky didn't know what to do next. Then he saw the cinema.
CINEMA
Erm ... Alexis?
Uh huh?
Would you like to see a film?
A movie? Oh, that's a nice idea, Rocky. But I've got to get back to Holly's. I'm expecting a call from – from a friend, you know? But thanks.

And after just two hours, Ricky watched Alexis walk away and disappear round a corner. He was frozen*. He was miserable. He was alone. And he felt like he was getting a cold. Two hours! He couldn't believe it. He didn't know what to think. Was she bored by him? Didn't she like him? Why didn't she stay longer? Why didn't she come to the cinema with him? A 'movie'! It sounded so much more romantic than a 'film'. He thought about the conversation and remembered every word.

Ricky sighed to himself. He was a disaster. Their meeting was a disaster. When he got home he said, 'I'm not feeling very well', and went to bed. His head was burning. And once again, he couldn't sleep.

On Monday morning, Ricky walked to school with slow, reluctant•
steps. He didn't want to see anyone.

'Everyone will know by now that I asked Alexis out•. Oh, why did I
do it? What was I thinking of? How could she like me? I'm nobody!'

He didn't look around when he entered the school but went straight
to his classroom. He didn't look up when his friends said hello or asked
about his weekend.

He thought everyone was looking at him, that they were all
laughing at him. In fact, only one person was looking. And that was
Holly.

During the maths lesson, Ms Cooke asked the type of question that only Ricky could answer. Everyone waited, but Ricky didn't say a word.

'What do you think the answer is, Ricky?' she asked.

Ricky didn't reply. He seemed to be studying the top of his desk.

Ms Cooke looked confused. This wasn't like Ricky at all.

'Erm, Ricky,' she said loudly.

Ricky looked up. Ms Cooke was staring● at him. Everyone was staring at him! He suddenly thought, 'Do they all know about me and Alexis?'

'Did you hear my question?' she asked.

'What question?' asked Ricky, and everyone laughed.

Everyone except Ms Cooke. And Holly.

As soon as the bell rang, Ricky rushed straight out of the classroom without saying a word. He walked quickly to the school gates and then started to run home. He didn't want to be with any of his schoolmates.

He was walking past the park when he heard a familiar voice. An American voice. It was Alexis! He could see her walking along one of the paths. She was on• her mobile phone. She didn't know he was there. He didn't want to listen to her private conversation, but he couldn't help it. He had no choice.

'Oh I know,' said Alexis, 'my cousin is really boring. It's the first time I've met her in years. She's a kind of● hippy ... yeah, she's a vegetarian and all that ... she's obsessed with recycling● and global warming● and all that stuff●...It's really boring!'

Ricky was surprised. He thought Alexis liked Holly. Everyone liked Holly.

'And then last weekend she had to do a school project and I went out for a walk with one of her friends ...'

Ricky's blood went cold. She was talking about him!

'Yeah, a boy ... but don't worry, you're still my boyfriend!'

So she had a boyfriend ...

'Anyway, I had a really boring time. It's such a boring little place here. And it's so cold!'

Ricky didn't listen to any more. He walked home, went up to his room, and for the first time in days turned on his computer. He played games, composed loud music, surfed the net. He didn't want to think about Alexis. He didn't want to think about anything at all.

The next day at school he noticed that Holly was looking at him. He looked at her. He felt sorry for her. She was so nice to Alexis, and Alexis said horrible things behind Holly's back. But they didn't talk to each other until the end of the day. He was walking across the school yard when Holly called his name.
'Ricky!'

Ricky turned. Holly smiled.

'That was really sweet of you to take Alexis around town on Saturday,' she said.

'Oh, that was OK,' Ricky replied.

'What was it like?'

'Oh, it was all right,' said Ricky.

'Did she say how amazing California is?' asked Holly.

'Er ... yes, she did,' said Ricky.

'And did she say how small everything is here?'

'Yes,' said Ricky, and smiled.

'She's hard work•, isn't she?' said Holly. 'I couldn't face• another day with her. That's why I invented that school project. I didn't have to do a project. You knew that, didn't you?'

And Ricky and Holly started laughing.

They walked home together – and never stopped talking for a moment.

'Do you know she's got a boyfriend?' asked Holly.

'Oh yes, she told me,' said Ricky, not quite truthfully.

'She's always talking to him on the phone.'

'I guess he's bigger and better than boys here,' Ricky said, and they both laughed again.

They stopped outside Holly's house. And as they were talking, the streetlights came on. Holly's brown hair glowed● in the light. Her blue eyes sparkled.

'She's going back with her parents on Friday. Do you want to come in and say goodbye?'

'No thanks, Holly,' said Ricky. 'I'll send her a text message!'

That night, Ricky had a dream.
He was walking through a strange city under a bright blue sky. There were tall shiny buildings on either side. And there were long shiny cars in the street.

He was walking beside a girl. She was a stranger to the city and he was showing her his favourite places. So they talked and laughed and the hours passed quickly.

Let's go this way.

Occasionally he tried to look at her – but when he turned towards her, she was always looking the other way. He could only see her hair, shining in the sunlight.

The sun was setting over the sea when they got to the beach. And as the sun was sinking on one side of the sky, the moon was rising on the other. They sat on the warm sands and watched the stars appear. The sea whispered quietly in the dark evening air.

And then Ricky looked at the girl again. This time she was drawing a pattern in the sand. No, it wasn't a pattern. She was writing her name.

He saw the letters H O L L ... and then the girl stopped and looked at him. She was smiling. She had a beautiful smile.

The next morning, Ricky woke up early. He immediately felt wide awake. He turned on his computer and quickly answered all his friends' questions about their maths homework. It didn't take him long. He got up from his desk and looked out of the window. It was still dark outside. He watched the postman delivering the mail. Then the first birds started singing.

'Why is everyone still sleeping?' he thought.

He wanted the day to begin.

At breakfast he chatted happily with Sonia and Jade. They were talking about boys, of course, but he didn't mind. It was interesting to hear what girls thought about boys.

David, Grace, Zadie and Jack were waiting in the school yard for the bell to ring.

'Have you seen Ricky?' asked David.

'No,' said Grace. 'He's been a bit weird lately, hasn't he?'

'A bit,' said David, 'but he helped me with my homework this morning, so he must be feeling better.'

'Where's Holly?' asked Zadie. 'She's late.'

'That's odd●,' said Grace. 'She always gets here early.'

'Look over there,' said Jack.

Ricky and Holly were walking through the school gates. They were talking and smiling happily.

'What do you think?' asked Jack.

'I think things are getting interesting,' said Grace.

After Reading

Understanding the story

1 What happens in the story? Number the sentences in the correct order.

a) ☐ Holly invites everybody to a fireworks party.
b) ☐ Alexis and Ricky go out together but the date is a disaster.
c) ☐ Alexis is lost and she asks Ricky for directions.
d) ☐ Ricky learns that Alexis is staying with Holly.
e) ☐ Ricky chats to Alexis at the party but he doesn't ask her out.
f) ☐ Ricky overhears Alexis giving Grace her mobile phone number.
g) ☐ Ricky sends Alexis a text message to ask her out.
h) ☐ Ricky wants to meet Alexis again but he doesn't know her name.

2 Circle the correct names.

a) **HOLLY / RICKY** always knows the answers to the questions in class.
b) **RICKY / JACK** is very kind and helps his schoolmates with their homework.
c) **ALEXIS / HOLLY** has got long blond hair and is very pretty.
d) **RICKY / JACK** is tall, tanned and good-looking.
e) **DAVID / RICKY** is a genius at maths and science.
f) **GRACE's / SONIA's** parents have got a shop.

3 What have you learnt about Ricky in this story? Talk about him with a partner. Then write a paragraph about him. These questions will help you.

What does he look like?
What have you learnt about his character?
What are his interests?
What kind of student is he?

4 Alexis is talking to her boyfriend on the phone. Tick (√) if the sentence is true for Alexis, put a cross (X) if it is false for her.

a) The people here in England are really boring. ☐

c) The town where I am staying is tiny. ☐

d) The weather is great. It's much warmer in England. ☐

b) The shopping malls are bigger and better in England. ☐

e) I'm having a fantastic time here in England. ☐

5 Complete Alexis's email to her boyfriend.

Hi ....,

How's everything with you? I'm having a really .... time here. Holly, my .... is a .... You know the type! She doesn't wear any .... and she wants to save the .... Yawn! Oh yes and she doesn't eat meat! She's a .... Her friends are all boring too.

Last week, we had a .... party. A lot of people came and it was OK. There was a big .... in the garden. They put a .... on top of it and burnt it.

On Saturday, Holly had to do a .... so I went out with a boy I met at the .... Don't worry!!! We had a boring time.

Missing you lots,
Alexis

After Reading

Vocabulary

1 Match the actions with the pictures.

a) paddle   **c)** explode

b) surf the net   **d)** wave

2 Look at the pictures and ask and answer questions with a partner.

What has exploded in the sky?
A firework.

3 Complete the speech bubbles with the opposites of the adjectives in brackets. Choose from the box below.

I like Steve. He's really (ugly) ....

We watched a really (boring) .... film on TV last night.

Fantastic! That's a (stupid) .... idea.

I hate this English weather! It's cold and (dry)............ .

I love your shirt, Ricky. It's (unfashionable) ....

Yesterday was just an (different) .... day until I met Alexis.

cool	ordinary	good-looking	brilliant	interesting	damp

4 When can you use these phrases? Match.

1 I'm a geek.

a) You want to ask somebody, "What is wrong?"

2 No way.

b) You don't think something is funny.

3 Hey, I was only kidding.

c) You think you are boring and unfashionable.

4 So, what's up?

d) You think something is not possible.

5 Very funny. Not.

e) You want to say something is OK or fine.

6 Sure.

f) You are joking.

57

After Reading

Grammar

Practise the Present Continuous for Future.

1 **What are the arrangements for the fireworks party? Complete the sentences with the present continuous form of the verbs.**

| wear | have | start | come | go |

a) Holly .... a party on Saturday.
b) The party .... at 5 o'clock.
c) Everybody from school ....
d) Ricky .... a purple shirt, blue jeans and a leather jacket.
e) The American girl .... to the party too.

Practise *Will*.

2 **Fill in the blanks with the correct form of the verbs below.**

| wear | be (x2) | go | not be |

Jade: Hey, Ricky, you don't usually go to parties.
Ricky: I know but I think this one .... interesting.
Jade: Who do you think .... there?
Ricky: Everybody from school I expect.
Jade: What are you going to wear?
Ricky: I'm not sure. Maybe I .... my purple shirt.
Jade: Cool! You look quite good in that.
Ricky: Do you want to come?
Jade: No, there .... anyone interesting there.
Ricky: What are you going to do tonight?
Jade: I think I .... to the cinema with Sonia.

58

Practise Reflexive Pronouns.

3 Complete the sentences with a reflexive pronoun (*myself*, etc).

a) Ricky walked home by .... last night.
b) Ricky's friends can't always do their homework by ....
   Ricky has to help them.
c) I have never been on holiday by ....
d) Holly made the cake ....
e) You have to collect the wood for the bonfire by ....
f) We got everything ready for the party by ....
g) My cat can feed ....

Practise the Present Perfect.

4 Complete the dialogue. Write questions and true answers for you. Use the present perfect with *ever* and *never*.

Ricky: Have you ever been to a fireworks party? (go to a fireworks party)
You: No, I've never been to a fireworks party. / Yes, I have.
Ricky: .... ? (buy any fireworks)
You: ....
Ricky: .... ? (light a firework)
You: ....
Ricky: .... ? (hear of Guy Fawkes)
You: ....
Ricky: .... ? (make a Guy)
You: ....
Ricky: .... ? (cook potatoes on a fire)
You: ....
Ricky: .... ? (eat toffee)
You: ....
Ricky: Well I hope you can come to our fireworks party next November 5th.

After Reading

Test

🎧 12 **1 Listen to the conversations and choose the correct picture.**

1 1 ☐   2 ☐   3 ☐

2 1 ☐   2 ☐   3 ☐

3 1 ☐   2 ☐   3 ☐

4 1 ☐   2 ☐   3 ☐

5 1 ☐   2 ☐   3 ☐

2 Read the sentences about the story and choose the best word (1, 2 or 3) for each space.

a) The story takes place in England in ....
   1 winter   2 spring   3 summer

b) The main character, Ricky, is very good at ....
   1 art and design   2 maths and science   3 French and Italian

c) Ricky meets an .... girl.
   1 African   2 Australian   3 American

d) Ricky is very kind and usually helps his friends with their ....
   1 homework   2 housework   3 girlfriend problems

e) Ricky and Alexis have a very .... date.
   1 frightening   2 interesting   3 boring

f) Ricky finds out that he gets on .... with Holly than with Alexis.
   1 better   2 worse   3 nicer

3 Look at the pictures on pages 50 and 51 with a partner. Ask and answer questions about Ricky's dream date with Holly.

What's the weather like?
It's warm and sunny.

Glossary

11 **a bit of a mathematical genius:** very good at maths
    hanging: resting
12 **blushed:** went red with embarrassment
    No way!: No he isn't!
    topic: subject
13 **actually:** really; in fact
    advice: ideas on how to solve a problem
    charge: ask for money
    pointed out: said a fact
    schoolmates: friends at school
14 **a bit of a hero:** very popular
    nodded: moved his head to say 'yes'
15 **represented:** was; meant
    whenever: when; every time
17 **bits:** pieces
    blazer: jacket
    damp: wet
    giggled: laughed
    set off: started to go towards
    turned up: put up
    whispered: said in a low voice
18 **kidding:** joking
20 **restless:** not relaxed; agitated
    what's up?: what's the problem?
21 **sitcom:** situation comedy; amusing TV serial
22 **flashy:** expensive and beautiful
    skyscrapers: tall buildings
    tossed and turned: moved around in bed trying to get to sleep
23 **paddling:** walking in low water
    rolled up: made shorter by turning up
24 **didn't mind:** didn't care

27 **fireworks:** a show of coloured lights, smoke, etc.
made an announcement: said an important thing
miserable: not nice or enjoyable
28 **groaned:** made a noise to say they weren't happy
just the same: nevertheless
planet: world
teasing: making fun of
veggie: vegetarian
29 **pounding:** banging
spinning: moving round and round
swallow: make food/liquid go down your throat
weird: strange
30 **get it:** understand it
31 **pleasant:** nice
trendy: fashionable; cool
32 **executed:** killed because of something bad you did
on death row: who will be killed
shaking: trembling; moving without control
35 **cute:** nice
38 **arrange:** make an appointment; decide a time, etc
contained: included; had
sleepless: not sleeping
worse: less good
40 **high street:** most important street in a town
shopping malls: shopping centres
41 **tiny:** very small
42 **frozen:** very cold
43 **asked Alexis out:** asked Alexis to go on a date
reluctant: when you don't want to do something
44 **staring:** looking without moving her eyes
45 **on:** (here) talking on

46 **a kind of hippy:** like a hippy
    global warming: phenomenon of the earth getting hotter
    recycling: using materials such as paper/glass again
    stuff: things
48 **I couldn't face:** (here) I didn't want to spend
    she's hard work: she's not easy to be with
49 **glowed:** shone
50 **occasionally:** sometimes
51 **setting:** (here) going down
    sinking: going down
53 **odd:** strange